In memory of
Helen Pearce & Mike Wrublewski OAM

www.thesymph.com

First published in the USA by Strategic Book Publishing and Rights Co.
Hardcover Edition 2012

Reprinted 2014

e^tv PUBLISHING
ONPAGE · ONSCREEN · ONLINE

PO Box 302 St Peters 2044
NSW Australia

www.etv.net.au

ISBN: 978-0-9925134-0-5

THE SYMPH
IN SEARCH OF HARMONY

Written by George Trad
Illustrations by Beniamino Bradi

Chapter 1 : The Loss of Harmony

Vivaldi the Violin of the String family loved music, but in the world of The Symph, music was forbidden. No one was allowed to play it any more because long ago it had led to trouble.

Vivaldi's parents told him stories of when the Conductor led the different families of The Symph; the Strings, the Brass, the Woodwind, and the Percussion together in harmony. The families came together as the Orchestra to play music – and it made everyone happy. Vivaldi loved these stories, but now it was all different. The Conductor had disappeared, the Baton was lost, and the Orchestra was no more. The families of The Symph were no longer in harmony – they were at war.

Sometimes Vivaldi and his friends in the Strings, the Viola, the Cello, and the Double Bass played music in secret. They dreamed of a time when there would be no more fighting between The Symph families and when the Evil One who took away their voices would be gone.

Everyone had heard rumours about what was happening in the lands of the Brass, and how they had joined with the Evil One. There were stories of instruments being captured by the Brass army and stripped of their voices.

"Why?" asked Vivaldi. "Who is this Evil One and why would he do such things?"

"The Evil One was jealous of the way the Strings were honoured and of the beautiful sounds that came from them without effort," explained Vivaldi's father. "The Evil One was once one of the Strings; a Piano, but everyone looked to us violins for leadership.

"Piano tried to steal the Baton and when the Conductor disappeared suspiciously, a feud broke out amongst the Strings and eventually the families of The Symph were torn apart by war. Now the Baton has been hidden and the Evil One's quest is to find it at all costs. The remaining Strings were the only family strong enough to stop him.

"Piano became the leader of Electronica when Moog and Synthesizer transformed him into Keyboard. With the help of the Electronica, Keyboard now had control of the Samplers. He made a deal with the Brass and had them believe that by stripping instruments of their voices and sampling them, they could control the Sacred Score and take over the entire world."

Vivaldi sighed a long note. He could not understand why a fellow String could be so wicked. "But what about everyone else?" he said. "Surely there were more in the Orchestra than just the Strings and the Brass?"

"The Percussion family was always wild and free, so they were immune to the Evil One's advances and the Woodwind lived far away in the high mountains and could not be approached," said Vivaldi's father. "It was the Strings who bordered the lands of the Brass, and felt the full might of the Evil One's sinister plans."

Chapter 3 : Attack of the Brass

One day when Vivaldi was playing with his friends a strange noise startled them. It was the Brass army and the Samplers attacking the lands of the Strings. They were blasting horrible sounds at everyone and trying to capture any instruments unable to defend themselves. Vivaldi and his friends hid as quickly as they could. "It's not fair," whispered Vivaldi. "Life shouldn't be like this."

"You're right," said his best friend, the Double Bass. "But what can we do?"

"I don't know, but we have to do something," said Vivaldi.

When the dust finally settled and the String warriors had driven the Brass off, Vivaldi vowed that one day all the families would play music together again. He would never rest until harmony was restored to the world of The Symph.

On a moonlit night soon after, Vivaldi sneaked out to begin his quest. To his surprise, he found the Viola, the Cello and the Double Bass waiting for him at the edge of the village.

"You didn't think we were going to let you have all the fun," said feisty Viola with a grin.

Vivaldi gave up trying to change their minds so together they set off for the lands of the Percussion.

"I've heard lots about their leader, Timpani," said Vivaldi. "If anyone can help us, he'll be the one."

"Then why hasn't he?" grumbled the Cello.

"Maybe he doesn't know what's happening. Or maybe no one has ever asked him," said Vivaldi.

CHAPTER 4 : MEETING OF TIMPANI

*T*he borderlands of the Percussion were covered with thick forest. It was hard to move silently through the dense undergrowth with branches and vines catching on their strings as they passed.

Suddenly appearing out of the trees came a band of Drums, Tambourines, Cymbals and many more of the Percussion family. The young Strings were surrounded.

The biggest and most frightening of all was a huge drum that stepped forward, towering above them and seeming to cover the whole sky.

"What brings the Strings to the land of the Percussion?" he boomed. The friends quivered, but then the huge drum laughed.

"Introduce yourselves," he boomed. "My name is Torelli the Timpani."

So, they were in the presence of the legendary Timpani! They all breathed a sigh of relief and told him their names.

"Splendid!" rumbled Torelli. "Let's make music!"

CHAPTER 5 : DANCE OF THE PERCUSSION

*T*he young Strings were astonished, but they soon found that music was alive and well in the lands of the Percussion. Everyone here played music and sang and danced without fear. It was part of their everyday life. Vivaldi and the others joined in with much joy and happiness.

After hearing about the Brass army and the capture of instruments, Torelli called for silence in order to make an announcement. "We will help you in your quest, Vivaldi the Violin. We must take the Sacred Score and go to the mountains of the Woodwind."

Vivaldi had heard of the Sacred Score from his parents, in whispers around the family home. He was excited to hear the Timpani speak of it and wondered why. He soon forgot about it as preparations with their new friends began.

The Strings now had a Percussion section and they set off the next day. Torelli himself joined the quest, along with his most trusted friends, the Tambourine, the Triangle and the Cymbal.

Chapter 6 : Woodwind to the Rescue

After many days of travelling they came to the foot of the mountains of the Woodwind. As they made their way across a stream an ambush of Brass soldiers appeared out of nowhere. They soon were fighting for their lives.

Suddenly the air was filled with the sound of a mighty windstorm. From above, a squadron of gliding Flutes, Piccolos, Clarinets and Oboes swooped down upon the Brass and drove them away. The Woodwind had come to the rescue.

*P*uccini the Piccolo stepped forward to greet the Ensemble of Strings and Percussion.

"Much time has passed since the Percussion has journeyed so far from their lands," piped Puccini as he peered at Vivaldi and his friends. "And in the company of Strings?" he added. "These are strange times indeed! We will take you to the Great Hall and the gathering of the Woodwind. You will tell our leader what brings your Ensemble to our lands."

CHAPTER 7 : GUARDIAN OF THE BATON

When they arrived at the Great Hall of the Woodwind a Bassoon sat at the front with many instruments gathered round. She was playing a low tune and all around her were listening with rapt attention as if memorising note for note. The Ensemble was drawn forward by the strange, deep sound.

The music stopped and Bassoon looked intently into each instrument before resting her steady gaze on Vivaldi. A shiver of recognition vibrated through his strings and Vivaldi was confused.

"Greetings to the guardian of the Baton," whispered the leader of the Woodwind.

Her greeting puzzled Vivaldi. The Baton had been lost when the Conductor disappeared. How could he be the guardian?

The Bassoon smiled. "Do not trouble yourself now, young Violin. All will be revealed in time. You must stay and prepare for what is to come."

*T*ime passed in the lands of the Woodwind. Vivaldi played with many other instruments and the Bassoon taught him about conducting and composition. He learnt more about the Orchestra and the history of The Symph.

They spent much time puzzling over the Sacred Score and filling in the missing parts, unknown and unplayed since the Evil One tried to steal the Baton. The Bassoon told him it was the key to defeating the enemy.

On some days he played with strange instruments called Outlanders, different from any instruments he had ever seen. They were homeless outcasts who roamed throughout the lands of The Symph but were always welcomed and sheltered by the Woodwinds. From them Vivaldi learnt the Blues, Country, Folk, Jazz and Rock & Roll. The Microphone even taught him Rap and Hip Hop.

Vivaldi made new friends and learnt many different songs and sounds.

One day Vivaldi and his close friends were playing some tunes together. He felt he had learned all he needed to know, and that it was time to continue their quest. Vivaldi stopped playing and turned to his friends. Just as he was about to share his decision, the Bassoon came in unexpectedly with some loud and noisy strangers. The Strings jumped back in alarm thinking they were being attacked. The Double Bass burst forward to protect them.

"Put away your Bow!" ordered the Bassoon. "These are our friends."

The Bassoon had brought instruments from the Brass family, led by Franz Haydn the French Horn. With him were the Trumpet, the Trombone and the Tuba. The Strings could not help being suspicious of these renegade Brass instruments suddenly in their midst.

It became clear that these Brass instruments were risking discovery by helping other families. They were ashamed of the members of the Brass who joined with the Evil One and wanted to help Vivaldi in the quest.

"We have seen what is happening at the Opera House," wailed Franz, "and how the voices of the instruments are being taken away."

These brave Brass instruments wanted to make a stand against what was happening to their family. They would fight for harmony and against everything the Evil One stood for.

The French Horn then spoke of Keyboard, and how the Samplers and other Electronica had power over all the other instruments.

It seemed there was no limit to the volume the Evil One could produce. Voices of the captured instruments were being recorded and stored on Discs and Drives. They were then replayed as Loops and used against anyone who opposed him.

After they had told the others as much as they could, the Brass played them many new pieces of music and filled in parts of the Sacred Score, which they knew was important to the quest.

The Bassoon waited, watched and listened. It was time to rehearse Vivaldi to see if he was ready to lead the Orchestra.

*T*he big day of the rehearsal arrived. Everyone was arranged in the chamber ready to play his or her part. The Percussion section lined up at the back, with the Brass and the Woodwind opposite the Strings.

Suddenly the walls started vibrating and a great booming sound burst through the Great Hall. It was as if the very foundations were being shaken to pieces. It was the Brass army using the pounding Loops from Electronica – the Ensemble had been betrayed.

As the Brass attacked, Vivaldi leapt to the front and began the opening melody of the Sacred Score. Everyone in the chamber joined in. They matched the enemy note for note as the tune built up and pushed the attackers against the wall. The Brass army and Electronica fled for their lives.

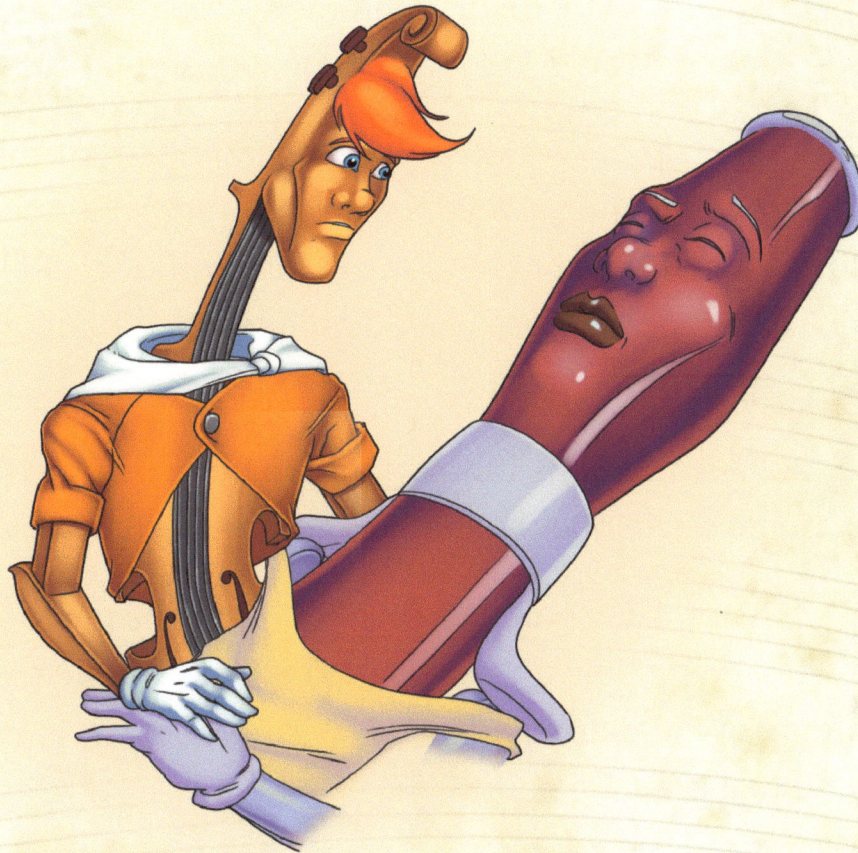

The tune of the Sacred Score soared through the final bars to come to rest with the sound of Vivaldi, the lone Violin. The enemy had been stopped once again and Vivaldi raced to the assistance of the shaken Bassoon.

"They have struck at the very heart of the Woodwind!" the Bassoon groaned. "The time has come to confront the Evil One!"

After their wounds were treated and their strength and resolve returned, the Ensemble prepared to leave for the lands of the Brass.

The group was made up of Vivaldi the Violin leading the Strings, Puccini the Piccolo with the Woodwinds, Franz Haydn the French Horn in charge of the Brass, and Torelli the Timpani behind the Percussion. The Outlanders knew a secret tunnel to the Opera House, so Guitar and Microphone joined with the Ensemble to show them the way.

The Bassoon took Vivaldi aside, away from the others, and pulled out a narrow wooden box. She opened the lid and revealed the lost Baton.

"Remember the Baton has no power of itself," she whispered. "The power comes from within the one who wields it! The first Conductor was the original guardian of the Baton and knew if it fell into the wrong hands then all would be lost.

So he battled against the Evil One and brought it here to the mountains of the Woodwind for safekeeping. Before he left he said a new Conductor would one day return to claim it. He had great hopes for you Vivaldi, for he was your grandfather."

Vivaldi realised that he had a great responsibility. He now knew he was the guardian of the Baton and must use it to bring harmony back to the world of The Symph. He would become the Conductor and lead the Orchestra to victory.

CHAPTER 13 : THE SECRET TUNNELS

The Ensemble began the journey in the early morning light. They moved steadily through the long day, at times rehearsing the part each would play in the coming battle.

As they reached the end of the mountain trail, the lands of the Brass stretched out before them. Vivaldi called for them to stop and rest.

The Outlanders had led them to the secret Tunnels of the Clef.

"This tunnel will take you directly to the Orchestra Pit of the Opera House," strummed the Guitar. "It is there you will make the final stand against the Evil One."

They entered the dark tunnels with Vivaldi leading the way.

After many twists and turns the Ensemble came upon the first of the dungeons. There were instruments locked behind bars and staring silently into space. They did not even notice the Ensemble passing by.

As they neared the Orchestra Pit, the Ensemble crept forward in readiness to play. Vivaldi moved to the front and drew out the Baton from where he had it hidden. They all gasped, as he held it up ready to count them in.

"One, and two, and three…..and four!"

28

The Ensemble began the opening bars of the Sacred Score and the music filled the Opera House. It challenged the sounds coming from Electronica out of PA and Speakers. The Evil One replayed Loops from the Discs and kept sliding up the volume.

At every change by the Ensemble, Keyboard responded and kept distorting the sound from the Speakers. The Ensemble did not give up. Vivaldi used the Baton to change the tempo. The sound of the Sacred Score swelled throughout the Opera House and into the tunnels and the dungeons below.

The music from the Sacred Score travelled down through the corridors to the dungeons. It swirled around the captured instruments and woke them from their deep stupour. They burst out of their cells into the Orchestra Pit and joined the Ensemble to make a full Symphony Orchestra.

As the music built to a crescendo the Evil One moved the Samplers into position.

Vivaldi could see what was happening. The whole Orchestra was going to be sampled and then saved to a Disc! He dashed onto the Stage and charged forward playing the solo from the Sacred Score directly into the Speaker.

The Speaker started to scream and whine uncontrollably. The squealing grew louder and louder until it blew up and all the Electronica were utterly destroyed. In all the confusion they did not see a small part of Keyboard disappear out through the Stage door.

As the smoke cleared, Vivaldi and the Orchestra began the Final Movement of the Sacred Score.

The Evil One had been defeated at last and could make music no more.

Chapter 16 : The Return of Harmony

From that day forward Vivaldi the Violin led the families of instruments, and as the new Conductor, showed them that harmony was the key to peace in the land of The Symph. Never again would the voices of instruments be taken away and used for evil purposes.

All instruments were treated equally and with respect and everyone was allowed and encouraged to play music. The best players and groups from all families journeyed to the Symphony Hall each year to play the Sacred Score and join with fellow instruments making up many other compositions.

On this day Vivaldi the Violin raised the Baton and began the first bars of a new song and a new beginning, for all the instruments and families, in the world of The Symph.

Lands of THE SYMPH

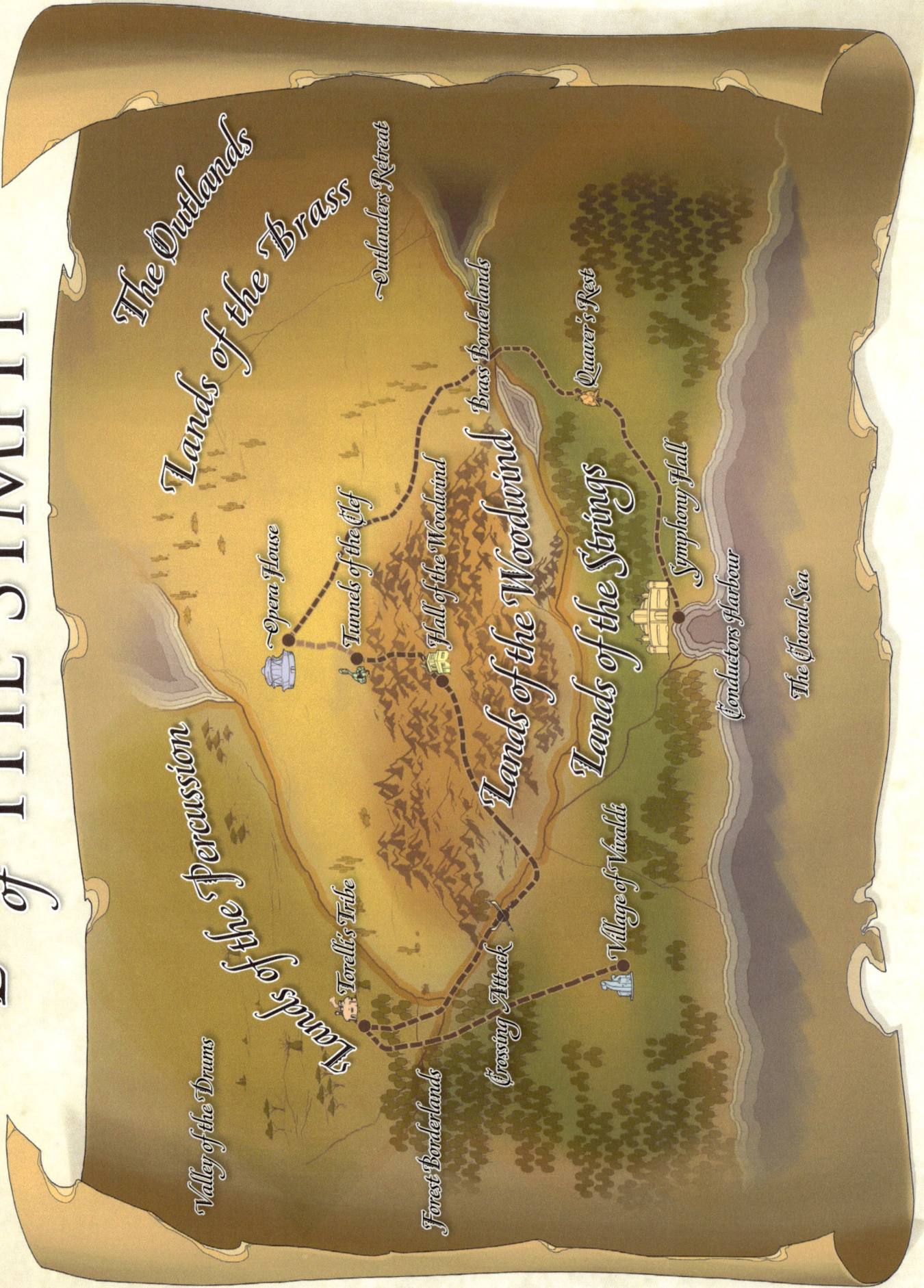

The Outlands

Lands of the Brass

Outlanders Retreat

Quaver's Rest

Brass Borderlands

Tunnels of the Clef

Hall of the Woodwind

Lands of the Woodwind

Symphony Hall

Opera House

Lands of the Strings

Conductors Harbour

The Choral Sea

Lands of the Percussion

Torelli's Tribe

Village of Vivaldi

Crossing Attack

Valley of the Drums

Forest Borderlands

Orchestra Key

Percussion

Brass

Woodwind

Strings